# Yes M'Lady

## At Home With The Ansons

## 1888 ~ 1900

GW00703223

# Yes M'Lady

## At Home With The Ansons

## 1888 ~ 1900

June Mary Harris

The Pentland Press Limited
Edinburgh  Cambridge  Durham  USA

First Published by
The Pentland Press Limited
Hutton Close
South Church
Bishop Auckland
Durham

ISBN : 1 85821 513 7

Typeset and Printed by
Lintons Printers, Crook, County Durham

*DEDICATED*
*TO THE MEMORY OF MY GRANDMOTHER*
*AND THE MANY HUNDREDS OF SERVANTS*
*WHO WERE THE MAINSTAY OF VICTORIAN*
*STATELY HOMES*

For every copy of this book sold £1.00 will be donated to the
Civil Service Benevolent Fund

# Contents

# About the Author

June Harris was born in 1930 at Andover, Hampshire, where she was brought up and has lived for lengthy periods.
In 1946 she joined the Civil Service as a shorthand typist. Her career spanned 42 years, firstly in the Secretarial and then in the Executive grades.

Family longevity has provided her with many interesting tales from the past, and several years ago she published in the *Hampshire County Magazine* stories about "Victorian Danebury" and "Wallop Baptists in Victorian Times".

More recently, she has compiled into a book, on behalf of her mother, the latter's girlhood memories of the First World War, which were published by the *Andover Advertiser* in 1995, under the title "Remembrance".

The author with her grandmother in 1937

# *Acknowledgements*

I wish to thank my mother for our many discussions about my grandmother's reminiscences, which have helped to keep these stories alive over the years.

I also thank my friends Joan Britton, Vivienne Faragher, Jean Dorrington, Trudi Morris, Iris Breese and Ruth Edwards for the great interest they took in my early attempts at putting the tales into writing.

# *Introduction*

I always enjoyed listening to my grandmother's reminiscences about life in Victorian stately homes. She had spent a number of years at the end of the nineteenth century as lady's-maid to the third Countess of Lichfield, had lived at Shugborough Hall, the Anson family's mansion in Staffordshire, and had visited a number of other great houses.

She was born in 1864 in the Wiltshire village of Newton Toney near Amesbury, the second daughter of Andrew and Elizabeth Philpott who named her Winifred Amy. The family moved into Hampshire when she was four years old, her father, who was a gardener, having obtained a better job at Danebury House near Stockbridge.

In those days, Danebury was famous both for the successes achieved by the horses trained there by John Day and ridden by Tom Cannon, and for its annual race meeting. The latter was a grand social event which took place in the summer and attracted large crowds of enthusiastic race-goers, including the Prince of Wales, later Edward VII. It is only in more recent times that the area has been recognised as an important Iron Age site.

The three Philpott children attended an Endowed School in the village of Nether Wallop, some two miles away. The school's benefactor had specifically stated in his will that girls were not to be taught too much. He feared that it would make them saucy, they would all want to be chambermaids, and there would be a dearth of cooks! Perhaps the school mistress overlooked this admonition when she taught the girls to sew, because it was grandmother's dressmaking skills which eventually enabled her to achieve a place as lady's-maid.

Very sadly, between 1881 and 1884, she lost her sister and both parents. She and her brother went to live with their relatives, Mr and Mrs George Legg, who ran a nursery garden next to the original All England Lawn Tennis and Croquet Club at Wimbledon. Taking advantage of her proximity to London, she decided to learn more about dressmaking at an establishment in the West End, and at that period stayed in one of the

Young Women's Christian Association hostels during the week, returning to Wimbledon for Sundays.

The YWCA aimed to help young women in business, and to provide them with accommodation which was both cheap and safe. The founders of the organisation had been greatly concerned that single ladies looking for lodgings, especially in London, could be lured into the "Bordellos" (as the Victorians called brothels) and forced into prostitution. Such places were illegal, of course, but existed nonetheless. Grandmother had personal experience of attempted procurement when an older woman followed her back to the hostel one evening. As she ran the last few yards to the front door, the woman started to give chase but disappeared quickly when the warden came out.

The tests set at the end of the dressmaking training included designing, cutting and making, in one week, a jacket and skirt for a friend who was willing to act as the model. In addition, certain special tasks had to be completed, such as cutting a specified number of buttonholes and working them in silk twist.

# A Place with Lady Anson

Grandmother achieved a good standard in the examinations, and was recommended by the tutor for an interview with Viscountess Anson whose personal maid was leaving her service.

Lady Anson, whose husband was the heir to the Earldom of Lichfield, preferred to engage her own dressmaker rather than have her clothes made at one of the couturier houses. She considered the latter were too expensive, and she also disliked the elaborate styles which were the vogue at that time. Since grandmother preferred to work on plainer garments and shared her Ladyship's views on design, she was offered the place as personal maid.

When she joined the Anson household in 1888, the family's London home was at 5 Granville Place, which is off Oxford Street in the area behind Selfridges, although that store was not opened until some years later. Viscount and Lady Anson had five children at that stage, the eldest being the eight year old Lady Bertha. There were two other daughters, Lady Mabel and Lady Violet, and two sons, Thomas (the next heir) and little Arthur ("Arty"). The domestic staff included a butler, housekeeper, cook, valet, governess, nanny, parlour maid, housemaid, nursery maid, kitchen maid, and two footmen.

As the lady's-maid, grandmother ranked as one of the Upper Servants. She was given a bedroom-cum-sewing room on the top floor of the house. It was comfortably furnished, but because it was near the roof and had a low ceiling, it was hot and stuffy in warm weather.

As well as dressmaking for Lady Anson and the three girls, her duties included personal attendance on her ladyship, with tasks such as helping her to dress, arranging her hair, and assisting with nursing if necessary. She was also required to accompany her on journeys and visits, and occasionally to undertake errands and convey messages.

She was absorbed into the daily life of the household quite quickly, getting along very well with the French governess, and forming a friendship with the housekeeper, Bessie Littlejohn, which lasted until the latter's death in about 1935.

Grandmother's relatives —
GEORGE LEGG,
Nurseryman of Worple Road,
Wimbledon

and his wife
ANNIE LEGG

# *Philly*

It was standard practice then for servants to be addressed by their surnames, but some employers preferred a less formal approach which could be achieved by inventing a diminutive of the name. Thus, Lady Anson dubbed grandmother "Philly".

Lady Bertha soon decided that Philly was to be her special friend, and often went up to grandmother's room for a chat. The latter was quite happy to talk as she sewed, but drew the line at entertaining the young lady's dog, especially when it jumped on the bed. "But mother doesn't mind him on her bed," protested Bertha. "Perhaps not, Lady Bertha, but I DO," grandmother replied. Bertha left her pet behind on all her future visits!

Philly was soon busy making new clothes for Lady Anson to wear during the London Season. Her Ladyship had been unable to attend all of the great events of the previous summer in honour of Queen Victoria's Golden Jubilee, because she had been pregnant with Arty who had been born at the end of July. This year she was looking forward to attending one of the Queen's famous "Drawing Rooms" at Buckingham Palace. These were afternoon Court receptions at which ladies were presented to the Queen. Once a lady had been honoured in this way, she was accepted as a member of Society and became eligible for further attendances at Court and invitations to other grand social functions such as balls, parties, etc.

Grandmother set to work with brocades, silks and velvets, which she stitched on her chain-stitch, single-thread, Wilcox & Gibbs hand-operated sewing machine. She told me that the early lock-stitch twin-thread machines exerted too much pressure on fine fabrics, causing garment seams to pucker.

It was the fashion for the bodices and skirts of dresses to be made as separates, thus enabling them to be mixed and matched. Lady Anson liked to have two differently designed bodices to each skirt, as an economical

THE THIRD COUNTESS OF LICHFIELD, c1900
Photographed in a braided, puff-sleeved bodice fashioned by Philly

way of ringing the changes. The bodice and skirt were belted together at the waist. Very slim waists were considered smart, and corsets were worn under the dress to make a firm silhouette. Some ladies, who thought themselves rather too portly, insisted on undergoing the painful procedure of getting their maids to tie the corset laces very tightly. Grandmother said that she was glad that she had no need to apply this "torture" to Lady Anson, who had a naturally small waist.

Dressing for presentation at Court was not entirely a matter of personal choice. There were quite a number of rules which had to be observed. The Débutantes, who were young single ladies being presented for the first time, had to wear white dresses, whilst other ladies were allowed to use coloured materials. The back waist of the skirt had to be fitted with a train at least two or three yards long. Ladies had to cover their hair with a veil held in place with a tiara, and, for those who had already been presented, the front of the hair had to be adorned with three ostrich feathers creating an effect rather like the plumes in the Prince of Wales' badge. (1) Gloves had to be worn, and a bouquet of flowers carried.

Lady Anson usually employed a hairdresser to set her hair for special occasions, but often complained about the heaviness of the resultant up swept coiffure, the lengthy process needed to achieve it, and the heat necessary to dry the hair. Grandmother described the dryer as a "kind of oven thing" into which the head was placed, but I think this must have been an early type of the familiar hood. One particularly hot summer morning, when her Ladyship's hair had been specially dressed, she decided that she simply could not face wearing it like that all afternoon. "Oh, do take it down, Philly." "Yes M'Lady." So grandmother unpinned the hairdresser's creation, removed all the pads which had been inserted to give a bouffant effect, and rearranged the hair into Lady Anson's normal style! The plainer appearance seems to have been perfectly satisfactory!

(1) Wilcox, R Turner, *The Dictionary of Costume*, published by Batsford, 1970.

# Shugborough and Holkham

By the middle of July, Lady Anson frequently said how glad she would be when it was time to go to Shugborough away from the stuffy London air. Viscount Anson's parents were both still alive then, so he and his family looked forward to August and September in the Staffordshire countryside as being "at home for the holidays."

Grandmother, too, came to enjoy staying at the old house, with its extensive grounds. Once again the room which she was given was on the top floor, but there was more space and, of course, the air was fresher. She was soon shown some of the interesting objects displayed in the house, and was fascinated by the room which was entirely devoted to Admiral Anson's circumnavigation of the globe in HMS *Centurion* from 1740-44. She told me that there was a model of his ship and a large collection of Chinese curios.

The general atmosphere at Shugborough was, of course, much more relaxed and she had a good deal of free time in which to explore the grounds, visit the Essex bridge, the "follies" such as the Octagon Tower and the Triumphal Arch, and the memorial to the cat which accompanied the Admiral on his long voyage. One of the housemaids, with whom she became friendly, suggested that they should get up very early one clear morning and go out to see the sunrise at Cannock Chase, then part of the estate. According to grandmother it was a wonderful sight, and the two of them always managed to make the excursion at least once a year.

She also experienced one of Staffordshire's less pleasant features. From time to time violent thunderstorms developed. The mining of iron ore in the district and the tall pottery chimneys of the nearby "Black Country" were alleged to attract lightning. During one of these bad storms trees in Shugborough park were struck and a number of cows were killed as they sheltered underneath from the torrential rain.

Back in London in October, she went shopping for cloth to make into

SHUGBOROUGH in the 1890s
Above - The Hall, Below - The Essex Bridge

winter garments. Her favourite store, which I think was called Robinsons, was in the Oxford Circus area. They had a wide range of materials and stocked a great variety of buttons, trimmings and other accessories. Her first task was to collect a good selection of samples from which Lady Anson could make a choice. Then she would return to the store to purchase the goods and would carry back the smaller items herself. The shop assistant would arrange delivery of larger parcels.

"Why don't you take the carriage?" her Ladyship would say sometimes. "No, thank you, M'Lady. It's quicker to walk." Traffic congestion in the West End was even worse then than it is today. All the vehicles were horse-drawn — buses, hansom cabs, carriages, delivery waggons. Sometimes horses would be frightened and rear up, possibly catching part of the harness around their legs. The wheels of one vehicle occasionally became entangled with those of another and had to be pulled apart. Manure was much in evidence, and crossing-sweepers performed an essential service.

Christmas was spent at Holkham in Norfolk, Lady Anson's childhood home. She was the youngest daughter of the 2nd Earl of Leicester son of the renowned agriculturist Thomas Coke of Norfolk. Her mother had died some years before and her father had married again. Every Christmas he and the Countess presided over a special gathering of his very large family. Holkham Hall was a big house, with plenty of room for all the Earl's children, in-laws, grandchildren, and the servants who accompanied them. In addition to the Christmas Day festivities, there was a great carol concert on Christmas Eve which everyone attended. Just after Christmas a grand ball was held for members of the family and invited guests, those servants not on duty being allowed to watch from the gallery. New Year's Eve was the occasion of the servants' ball, at which all the visiting servants as well as those employed in the Hall and on the estate were welcome. It was always opened by Lord and Lady Leicester who stayed for the first dance. His Lordship partnered the housekeeper, and Lady Leicester the butler.

The Rector of St Withburga's parish church seems to have been a kindly

This lady and gentleman are thought to be the widowed ISABELLA ASH, who was the gate-keeper at Shugborough Lodge, and her brother-in-law THOMAS ASH, a general labourer.

A group of Philly's fellow servants

Individual
photographs of
some of Philly's
fellow servants

Individual
photographs of
some of Philly's
fellow servants

More of Philly's
fellow servants

and reasonable man. At that time Anglican clergymen were somewhat aloof and inclined to be intolerant of non-conformists, but he chatted personally to all the visiting servants and invited them along to his services, regardless of denomination.

The Ansons usually stayed for several weeks, and, once again, grandmother had free time. The State Rooms of the Hall were open to the public on certain days, and she helped to conduct some of the guided tours, although she found them a bit worrying. "People would touch things," she said, and she was afraid that something valuable would be broken. Her favourite spot was the library, which she was allowed to use before breakfast whilst the household staff were cleaning. During these early morning sessions she read a volume which she described as "a wonderful book about the Protestant martyrs". I think that this must have been a complete edition of Foxe's *Actes and Monuments*, as compared with the popular, very abridged version, which she had probably read previously.

# Travelling

There was more visiting in the spring when the Ansons went to see relatives in Ireland. His Lordship's maternal grandparents were the first Duke and Duchess of Abercorn. His uncle had succeeded to the title several years earlier, but his grandmother was still alive. So the Abercorn's estate at Baron's Court, Omagh, County Tyrone, was on the Anson's itinerary, and another destination was the home of Lady Anson's brother-in-law and sister, Lord and Lady Leitrim, at Mulroy, County Donegal.

All this travelling involved long journeys by rail, sea crossings, and horse-drawn carriage rides. It was on a train journey that grandmother decided that diamonds are not necessarily a girl's best friend. It was the custom for the maid to take charge of the jewel case when she accompanied her employer on a journey, and grandmother was sitting with her Ladyship's case on her lap. She was in a second-class carriage, whereas Lord and Lady Anson were travelling in a first-class compartment in another part of the train. She noticed that one of the men in her carriage kept looking intently at the case, and was alarmed at the prospect of his attempting to snatch it from her. There was no corridor link between the first and second classes, so she waited until the train pulled into the next station. Then she jumped out and ran along the platform to the Anson's compartment, opened the door and thrust the case at them, saying "You'll have to take this. There's a man in my carriage who has his eye on it!" "That's all right, Philly", replied his Lordship calmly, "put the case in with us." I don't think that she ever carried it on a train again.

An Irish country road in a remote, mountainous spot, was the scene of another nasty scare. Grandmother had ignored Lady Anson's advice not to go very far from the house in which they were staying, without a companion. Instead she had asked an estate coachman to take her shopping in one of the villages. On the way back the driver halted the horse and carriage at the foot of a very steep hill, but made no attempt to explain why. She began to feel very uneasy and to fear that she might be the target of an ambush.

There had been "troubles" in Ireland for a long time, but in 1882 a particularly notorious incident had occurred in Phoenix Park, Dublin, when two British officials had been waylaid and murdered by members of the Fenian Brotherhood whose sworn objective was to overthrow English rule in Ireland. Now she realised why Lady Anson had warned her not to go out alone. After about five minutes of this silent halt, she asked the driver anxiously, "Why have you stopped? Why don't you go on?" She was extremely relieved when he answered, "Horse has to get his wind to get up the hill."

# *Rupert*

Lady Anson's sixth and last child, Rupert, was born in November 1889. He seems to have been a delightful baby and a favourite with the whole household. His parents invited Donald Alexander Smith (later Lord Strathcona) to be his Godfather. This gentleman was a pioneer financier who was honoured for his services to Canada, especially his enterprise and persistence in backing the construction of the Canadian Pacific Railway, the first permanent overland route to link the country's Atlantic and Pacific coasts. It seems likely that he was a business associate of Lord Anson who was a director of several banks including the old National Provincial, the Nat part of the present NatWest. The invitation probably set the seal on a partnership of new money and old nobility typical of the era.

He was very generous towards his little Godson, making a financial settlement which Rupert would inherit on his 21st birthday. "When he grows up, Rupert will be richer than any of us," Lady Bertha would say to grandmother sometimes. Whether or not her prediction came true I have no idea. The catastrophic events of the twentieth century, particularly the two World Wars and the Depression, have depleted and often completely wiped out so many fortunes.

Every time Rupert's Godfather visited the family he gave a sovereign (a gold coin valued at £1) to each of the other Anson children. Lady Bertha saved hers until she had enough to buy a pretty blue brooch which she had spotted in the window of a London jeweller's shop. "Please take me along to buy it, Philly. It costs eight guineas (£8.40) and I have saved the money, but when I go shopping with mother she always says there isn't time to stop!" It was not the custom in aristocratic families for girls and young unmarried women to wear much jewellery, however highly placed or wealthy their parents might be. Small brooches and simple necklaces were allowed, however, so grandmother agreed to take Bertha along to the shop. There, much to the latter's delight, the coveted brooch was still in the window and had not been bought by someone else.

(above) This little boy is thought to be the HON. RUPERT ANSON photographed in 1890. Interestingly, he is wearing rompers instead of a frock which was the usual attire for baby boys at that time. Possibly his garments were also designed and made by Philly.

(left) Three little friends from the estate

# Something Old, Something New

Lady Anson's Court dresses were remodelled following the season in which she had first worn them. The train was detached from the skirt and the material used to make a second bodice. Then she was able to wear the dresses as Tea Gowns on afternoons when she was entertaining at home or went to visit other ladies. An advantage of work done on the chain-stitch machine was that it could be unpicked very easily. Once a thread had been snipped, the stitches unravelled quickly, in the manner of knitting.

One brocade dress which underwent this transformation had a charming design of gold lilies of the valley on a cream background. As these flowers were grandmother's favourite, I think that she must have influenced the choice of material. A piece of it survived until the 1940s amongst the off-cuts which she had collected, and she gave it to me to make into a cushion cover. A similar fate befell two pieces of thick black silk. One was of the moiré water-marked type which had originally been made into a large bow fitted on to the back of a skirt as a mini-bustle. The other was a ribbed silk which had been part of the skirt of another dress. My smart cushion covers wore very well for some years, but eventually split and had to be discarded.

"You can have this, Philly," her Ladyship would say about garments which she no longer required. Grandmother was rather smaller, so she often altered them to fit herself, especially those made from velvet. She kept the ones for which she did not have an immediate use. Some she restyled at various times over the years; others she unpicked to make into clothes for her daughters.

# Worrying Events and Sad Ones

Lady Anson was inclined to worry, whereas her husband was apparently the essence of the unflappable Englishman. She was most alarmed on an occasion when a large crowd gathered in Hyde Park to voice workers' grievances about their conditions. After listening to speeches, which were no doubt intended to arouse as much indignation as possible, the protesters marched to Marble Arch and down Oxford Street. The housekeeper, Bessie Littlejohn, brought news via the grapevine. "They say they're going to the Palace," she told grandmother. "What's the good of that?" replied the latter. "The Queen's probably at Windsor." "Oh dear, do you think we ought to go to Shugborough?" asked her Ladyship anxiously. More than one nineteenth century European revolution had been sparked off by an angry crowd storming a royal palace. "Certainly not," was his Lordship's answer. "There isn't any danger."

Her daughters' riding lessons were amongst her Ladyship's other worries. Her husband had insisted that the girls must be taught to ride, but she was not at all happy about their doing so. "It's dangerous, Philly," she would say. Her fears seemed justified on the afternoon that a terrific thunderstorm broke whilst the young ladies were out with the riding master in Shugborough Park. She was extremely nervous that the ponies might be frightened and bolt, throwing off their riders. His Lordship's repeated assurances that the riding master was a very reliable horseman, who would ensure that they all came home safely, did little to calm her until, at last, four soaking wet riders appeared.

The year 1892 appears to have been one of mourning, which probably accounted for some of the pieces of black silk and velvet which came into grandmother's possession. Queen Victoria's grandson, the Duke of Clarence, second heir to the throne, died in January; a very sad event for which she ordered a period of Court mourning.

Her Ladyship's brother-in-law, the Earl of Leitrim, died during the year, and his Lordship lost his father, the 2nd Earl of Lichfield, so there were two spells of family mourning. Lord and Lady Anson were now the 3rd Earl and Countess of Lichfield, and the courtesy title of Lord Anson was passed on to their schoolboy son Thomas.

The Dukedom of Marlborough passed to another generation as well. The new Duke, the 9th holder of the title, was his Lordship's first cousin. The 8th Duke had been married to his Lordship's aunt, Albertha, Lady Blandford, but had been so unkind to her that she had been obliged to divorce him, which was very much an action of last resort in those days. Grandmother understood from Lady Lichfield that the then Lord Blandford had shown physical violence towards his wife, before deserting her for another woman. Following the attack, she had sought refuge with the Ansons who were appalled by his conduct. "We couldn't possibly let her go back to him, Philly," her Ladyship had said. Queen Victoria had been very sympathetic, allowing Lady Blandford to continue to receive invitations to the Court, a privilege normally withdrawn from people who divorced.

# Troublesome Cooks!

At Holkham the servants were getting out of hand. One of the New Year's Eve balls had ended in drunken revelry, and the very strong ale brewed by the cook had been blamed for the fiasco. The following year this particular beverage had been banned by a very annoyed Lord Leicester. Below-stairs some of the staff were upset by his ruling, and had their revenge at the carol concert. During the First Nowell, they were singing with great vigour, led by the cook who was beating time:

> *"No ale, no ale*
> *No ale, no ale*
> *What shall we do without our ale?"*

Later that evening, in reply to a remark from her ladyship about the high-spirited singing, grandmother couldn't resist saying "Yes, M'Lady, but you should have heard WHAT they were singing!"

Lord Leicester had no intention of relenting and the ale stayed banned for good, but at Christmas 1893 the servants had something different to interest them. The newly married Duke and Duchess of York (afterwards George V and Queen Mary) had accepted an invitation to the Grand Ball. The gallery that evening was soon filled with household and visiting staff eager to see the beautiful young Duchess.

The cook at the Anson's new London home was causing problems, too. They had moved from Granville Place to No 38 Great Cumberland Place a short distance away, and their recently employed cook was bullying the kitchen maid to an extent which alarmed the other members of the staff. None of them could persuade her to change her ways, and it was evident that Lady Lichfield would have to be informed. Grandmother undertook this task since she was the only one in a position to approach her Ladyship informally. "Oh dear, and she's such a good cook, Philly. I don't want to lose her. Do you think it would help if I had a word with her?" "Well, M'Lady, something will have to be done." The "word" was effective. The bullying stopped.

# *Invitations*

From time to time the Ansons received invitations to visit friends, and grandmother recalled staying at Harewood House in Yorkshire, Ashridge House in Hertfordshire, Ockham Park in Surrey, and Muckross House in Killarney. She disliked the former, which was the home of the Earl and Countess of Harewood. According to her it was a dark, grim place. Ashridge, on the other hand, was a much pleasanter house. The owners were Lord Brownlow and his wife Adelaide, who were noted for their kindness and hospitality.

Lord and Lady Lovelace lived at Ockham Park. He was the grandson of Lord Byron, and his very interesting collection of memorabilia associated with the poet was displayed in the house. The friendship between the Ansons and the Lovelace family developed into a closer relationship. In 1895 Lord Lichfield's sister, Lady Edith Anson, married Lionel King-Noel, Lord Lovelace's half-brother and heir to the earldom.

Killarney was grandmother's favourite spot. She was entranced by its magnificent scenery of mountains, lakes, fells and cascading waterfalls, and often spoke of its beauty. Muckross House, a Victorian mock-Elizabethan mansion, was built in 1840 for Henry Herbert, the Member of Parliament for Kerry. Over the years the family had entertained many guests there, including Queen Victoria. Grandmother took full advantage of her opportunities to walk through the lovely gardens and alongside the lakes, and to make jaunting car trips further afield.

An invitation which was not accepted came from Russia. Tsar Alexander III died in 1894 and was succeeded by his son Nicholas II. Later that year, the latter married Princess Alix of Hesse, a grand-daughter of Queen Victoria. Their coronation took place in Moscow in May 1896. These events were marked by a series of lavish entertainments, and the Russian nobles appear to have ensured that as many members as possible from the aristocratic families of other countries were asked to at least one special function.

KILLARNEY IN THE 1890s
(Above) Muuckross House, (Below) The Rapids, Old Weir Bridge

The Torc Cascade, Killarney

"His Lordship has decided that we shall not be going." Lady Lichfield told grandmother. "He says that Lady Blandford (who had also been invited) must do as she pleases, but apart from the expense, which he feels that we cannot afford, he considers that we could not possibly support such a cruel regime."

Some of the expense to which his Lordship referred was occasioned by the Russian nobles' practice of exchanging valuable gifts with their guests. Lady Blandford did attend, and the maid who accompanied her received a present from their hosts as well. It was a beautiful emerald brooch. "But what shall I do with it, Miss Philpott?" she said as she showed it to grandmother. "I can't wear it here, it's much too valuable." "Well you will either have to sell it or hide it away somewhere," was the latter's rather waspish advice!

Upper Wharfedale, Yorkshire in the 1890s
The Strid

# Tragedy and near Disaster

The summer of 1895 was overshadowed by the tragic death in July of Lady Evelyn Anson, Lord Lichfield's youngest sister. He was a member of a very large family, so that Evelyn, who was only 21, was closer in age to his eldest daughter than to himself. She caught measles from one of the housemaids at her mother's London home. This infectious disease often reached epidemic proportions before immunisation became possible. It was commonly contracted in childhood, when recovery was normally achieved within a few weeks, but the illness was much more serious in adults. Regrettably, this was the case with Lady Evelyn, who developed pneumonia for which there was no antibiotic cure at that time. The only hope lay in very careful nursing and the patient's own strength.

A tearful Lady Bertha shared her anxiety with Philly. "Poor Evie" was a big sister rather than an aunt to her. The doctors made strenuous efforts to save Evelyn's life, including, according to grandmother, the use of ice in a desperate attempt to reduce her soaring temperature. But it was to no avail, her heart was not strong enough to overcome the crisis. It was a very sad time for all the family and the two households. Fortunately, the housemaid recovered, but she must have been very upset when the bad news was broken to her.

Lord and Lady Lichfield decided to take a holiday in France during the early months of the following year. Various French resorts had been popular with English visitors for some time. Queen Victoria favoured Nice, the Prince of Wales liked Biarritz, and tourism in Cannes owed its beginnings to Lord Brougham, but accommodation in these places was costly. Lord Lichfield, therefore, accepted an offer of a villa in the rather remote little town of Pau which was reputed to have a mild winter climate. It is about 65 miles inland from Biarritz in the foothills of the western Pyrenees.

They were accompanied by his Lordship's valet and Philly. The boys were at school, and the girls were left at home in charge of the governess. One of the drawbacks of staying in a quiet backwater soon became apparent, however. No one, not even the domestic staff at the villa spoke any English. Although this would have given her Ladyship an opportunity to practise the French which she had learnt as a girl, any enjoyment she might have derived from that was short-lived because she developed German measles.

She was quite ill, the French maids were terrified of the "fever" and would not go into her room, and there was no English doctor for miles. Grandmother had to look after her, fetch her food from the kitchen, and clean out her room. She was cross with the housemaid and bullied her into fetching a broom. She was even more cross with his Lordship for bringing them to such an outlandish place. With his sister's death still a painful memory, she persuaded him that her Ladyship must have medical attention as soon as possible, and that the quickest way of getting it was for him to return to London to fetch the family's own doctor. There were no reliable international telegram or telephone services in those days, let alone all the modern communications to which we are accustomed.

Happily, Lady Lichfield recovered, but the doctor's fees increased the cost of a near-disastrous holiday. "I don't think we shall ever come here again," her Ladyship said one day when she was getting better. "I should hope not, M'Lady," replied grandmother who never made another visit to the Continent (and I rather doubt if her Ladyship did either!)

# Happier Times

The 1897 season was extremely busy, with all kinds of events and functions being held to celebrate Queen Victoria's Diamond Jubilee. The following year was Lady Bertha's "coming out", and grandmother made her a beautiful débutante dress. The main material had to be the customary white, but the rules did allow for the train to be lined with a colour, and Lady Bertha accepted Philly's suggestion that this should be pink.

"Now I have to have flowers," Bertha said as the great day drew near. "What sort of flowers do you think I should have?" "I should like you to have pink May blossom," grandmother replied, and she possibly asked her relative, Annie Legg, who ran the Worple Road florist shop in Wimbledon, to help with making up the bouquet.

I do not know if the Queen was there herself when Lady Lichfield took Bertha along to present her at Court for the first time, or whether the Princess of Wales (later Queen Alexandra) was deputising. The "Drawing Room" experience must have been nerve-racking for the young ladies, in spite of the hours they had spent practising deportment, walking sedately in Court dress, holding the train over the left arm, and the bouquet in the right hand, letting the train drop to the floor at the correct moment, and making the deep curtsy to the Queen or Princess.

After the presentation came the social round of balls and parties, for which grandmother made Lady Bertha another lovely dress. Imagine her delight when she overheard the latter telling admiring friends that Philly was not just a dressmaker but a designer as well.

His Lordship agreed to interviews and photographic sessions with a local Staffordshire newspaper the *Mercury*. In its edition of 7 April 1899 the paper published a long article and some excellent photographs in a special supplement, a copy of which grandmother kept as a souvenir. * The article contains vivid descriptions of the Shugborough estate, the Hall and the
*See Appendix Two

LADY BERTHA ANSON in 1898
wearing a dress which Philly had designed and made for her

LADY BERTHA ANSON in 1898
wearing another of Philiy's creations

grounds, and details of the Anson's family history. There are photographs of Lord and Lady Lichfield themselves, and pictures of some of the principal rooms of the house.

No doubt there was a great deal of feverish activity prior to the arrival of the reporter and photographer, with all the maids and footmen cleaning, polishing, dusting and making sure that everything was in exactly the right position. Outside, the gardeners would have been busy tidying up the grounds.

The photograph of the Saloon shows all the paintings hung in a very straight line and the chairs have been carefully spaced. According to the article, the picture which had pride of place was an engraving of Queen Victoria with her mother. The Queen had presented it to his Lordship during her Diamond Jubilee year, as a memento of a visit which she and her mother had made to Shugborough in 1832.

Lady Lichfield's boudoir, with which Philly would have been well acquainted, has a less formal appearance. The article describes it as "a cosy and comfortable room arranged in the best taste". Especially noticeable are the family photographs, of which there are at least seven on display.

A BREAK FROM LADY'S MAID'S DUTIES - A Holiday at Lowestoft
(Above) Philly captioned this picture 'Walk in Belle Vue Park'
Could she be the lady hidden behind the sunshade?
(Below) Royal Place and Pier

(Above) LOWESTOFT in the 1890s
(Below) The South Esplanade

# A Home Of Her Own

Grandmother told me that she had very much enjoyed the years that she had spent with the Ansons, she was glad to have had the opportunity to travel, and to meet so many people. Eventually, however, she began to feel that she really wanted a home of her own. At the beginning of this century there were no retirement pensions and no National Health Service. It was normal then for women to seek security through marriage.

She explained that she had been engaged to a young man when she was in her early twenties, but the relationship had not developed as she had hoped. Her marriage to my grandfather, Ralph Cable, had come about through her friendship with his mother, who had been her Sunday School teacher. She had kept in touch with the family and had visited them occasionally over the years. Originally, they had lived in the Hampshire village of Over Wallop, but Ralph and his mother had moved to the small market town of Andover following the death of his father a few years earlier, and the former had set up in business there as a carpenter and wheelwright.

He and grandmother had agreed that they would marry in the autumn of 1900, although she was reluctant to tell Lady Lichfield about her planned departure. However, she wrote to him during September to tell him that her Ladyship had said that "if I could make her a bodice and do up two dresses I could have the wedding from No 38" (Great Cumberland Place)

Lady Bertha was rather put out. "I do think that it's inconsiderate of you leaving now just as I was planning my wedding," she complained. Grandmother explained that it was probably her last chance to have a home of her own. "Oh, I would have looked after you and found you somewhere to live, Philly." "I'm sure that you would, Lady Bertha, but living on my own in retirement would not be the same as having a family around." She was puzzled about Lady Bertha's wedding plans, because she had not heard anything about an engagement. When she mentioned this to Lady Lichfield, the latter exclaimed brightly, "Oh, Bertha's looking for a husband." "I hope she finds one, M'Lady." The planning was evidently of the advanced variety!

Somehow over the next few weeks she managed to make herself a wedding dress, which was of purple silk with a white pin stripe. Hopefully, she also completed Lady Lichfield's bodice and dresses, but I suspect that some other jobs may not have been finished. Writing to grandfather at the end of September she said, "The work keeps coming but I doubt if I shall get through it!"

The wedding took place at the Presbyterian Church, Marylebone, on 18 October, and the reception was held at the Anson's London home. Lord and Lady Lichfield, their daughters, and the members of the household were present, and his Lordship made a short speech. It was time for Philly to say, "Goodbye, M'Lady."

PHILLY
at the time
of her marriage

RALPH CABLE -
Philly's husband and the
author's grandfather -
photographed in 1900

# *Epilogue*

Grandmother started married life in an old cottage close to a public house and next door to grandfather's workshop. Their elder daughter, my Aunt Evie, was born in 1901, and named after the young Lady Evelyn whose life was lost. Two years later the family moved into a house which grandfather had built in a part of Andover which was just being developed. My mother, their second daughter, was born in 1906.

There were occasional exchanges of letters with Lady Lichfield and Lady Bertha. Grandmother was invited to the latter's wedding in 1902, but unfortunately was not able to attend. Her last meeting with Lady Lichfield was early in the thirties. On a sudden impulse, whilst she was in London shopping with my aunt, she decided to call upon her Ladyship. The latter was very pleased to see them, and told grandmother that she had special memories of their time together.

Grandfather died in 1952, but grandmother lived on until she was 104 in 1968. When the old home was turned out I came across a poem which she had copied on to paper bearing the address of that villa in Pau. It is entitled "My Own Fireside", and these lines from it must have echoed her feelings for a long time afterwards:

> *Let others seek for empty joys*
> *Whilst far from fashion's idle noise*
> *I while the wintry eve away*
> *And marvel how I e'er could stray*
> *From thee — MY OWN FIRESIDE.*
> *Oh may the yearnings fond and sweet*
> *That bid my thoughts be all of thee*
> *Thus ever guide my wandering feet*
> *To thy heart-soothing sanctuary.*
> *What e'er my future years may be*
> *Let joy or grief my fate betide*
> *Be still an Eden bright to me*
> *MY OWN — MY OWN FIRESIDE*

# *APPENDIX ONE*

## *Letters from Philly to Ralph*

Shugborough
Saturday morn

My dearest Ralph

I have just received
your letter and am so sorry
that I did not make things clearer
to you. I daresay my last letter
was very stupidly put together
I was sorry after it had gone
that I had written it just when
I did for I had just had 2 or 3
different interviews with L^dy
and felt so worried & vexed but
thought I must let you have a
line to say I could go to J^d.
This week I have arranged to
go up on Monday next to 38
and I thought I would just run
down to Wim don Tuesday to hear
what they said and leave it
open with L^dy till Tuesday night
whether I should stay on at 38 or

not. The fact of the matter is
that when I told her I couldn't
stay down here till she came
back she wanted to know where
I was going to be married and
I said in London probably and
she said rather grudgingly I
could stay at 38 if I could make
her a bodice and do up 2 dresses
which of course means that I
must work every moment
hard to get done with all
this turning out & packing
up. and I thought if I could
manage at Wimbledon I would not
stay there at 38 only just to
pack up of course there are
things I must do for myself
I have never had any idea of
a grand affair as I don't want
it but it seems too hard to have

keep rushing on to the last minute you've no idea what they are but I shall be at St Cumb Pt on Wednesday to see you there when you come up — Thanks very much dear for yr letter on Wed last — I felt it a great comfort to me for it made me feel that you could to a certain extent understand & sympathize with me for it is so difficult to stick to the work as I have had to & the people here are so kind and all so so sorry I'm going away and I've not had time hardly to see them the thought

2. of being with you and having some rest & peace amply makes up for any regrets at parting with old friends I have had several nice presents and can't help feeling touched at all the kindly feeling that is shown to me if only p[?]g

was it so determined to get such
a lot done it has been so diffic
to prepare for giving every thing
up to her which takes place today
How dear I hope I have made
this so that you will see a little
what to do I don't know when they
are coming back here I think the
5 or 6 of Oct.d if she can get settled
with a maid with fond love
hoping you will forgive me for
troubling you so will try to make
up when I do get free
lots of kisses
                Ever Yr loving
                      Dennis?

excuse hasty letter

38 G.t Cumberland Place
London W
Wednesday

My Dearest Ralph
Just a line to
tell you that I have
sent off three boxes
today I don't know where
you will put them but
I thought perhaps you
could have them in
the shop it doesn't
matter a bit as long

as they are in the
dry as the boxes are
not much good.
I am so glad to get
them off before they
got up here it has
been quite a business
turning out every
place I have another
small hamper with
china in it beside
the one you saw

but if we can't take
every thing I can leave
it with Bessie for
a time Ld Ly & Ld He have
got up here & His Ld Ly
is here all the week
as well it is too bad
of them shall be so
glad when I'm away
what summer
weather we're having
I hope it will last
a bit longer I shall be

looking for a line from
you soon dear good bye
for the present with
fondest love & kisses
From
Your ever loving
Winnie

My love to your Mother

# APPENDIX TWO

## Extracts from an article in the Mercury, 7th April, 1899

# Shugborough Hall

The Rt. Hon. Earl of Lichfield
and the Countess of Lichfield

The Seat of the Right Honourable the Earl of Lichfield, at Shugborough, is well known, not only to the inhabitants of the county generally, but to the thousands of excursionists who are permitted every summer to visit the beautiful park, which is situated but a few minutes' walk from Colwich, and close to the villages of Great and Little Haywood. It forms, in fact, a central position between Ingestre on the north, Beaudesert and Wolseley on the south, Blithfield on the east, Tixall on the west, and Teddesley on the south-west. The estate, which comprises many hundred acres of beautiful park-land, noble woodland scenery, and broad meadows, extends from the high road at Haywood on the one side to the main road from Lichfield to Stafford on the other, edged by the heath-clad hills of Cannock Chase from Oak Edge to Milford. It is watered by the rivers Trent and Sow, which wind gracefully through the estate, and add greatly to the charm of its surroundings. The mansion itself occupies a central position in the park and commands an uninterrupted view in every direction. The manner in which the gardens, shubberies and pleasure grounds are laid out, with a keen eye to effect and beauty, and in compliance with the requirements of modern taste, furnishes everything that can be desired.

That a place of such importance, containing besides its natural beauties, so many points of interest connected with the lives of those who have in the past been its fortunate possessors, has a history of which it may well be proud, goes without question. From the time when the old episcopal palace belonging to the See of Lichfield and Coventry, stood here in 1085, until a more modern date, its history may be easily traced in all the old county chronicles, and with these matters it is not our present province to deal. It is sufficient to state that the original name given to the estate is said to be that of Sowborough or Sowburrow, and that it passed into the hands of different possessors until it finally reached those of the Anson family, one well known in the county for many generations

In approaching the mansion from the grounds, the hall has a most imposing and attractive appearance. Although it is of no particular style of architecture, it is undoubtedly a noble pile of buildings, the walls being faced with wide slates painted, while the mansion has a fine centre and handsome portico, with two semi-circular wings. The portico, which is reached by a flight of broad steps, is ornamented with eight fluted ionic columns, and opens into a spacious hall, from which branch off corridors on either side. All the rooms on the ground floor have an appearance of elegance and comfort, being richly decorated, while the furniture, pictures and artistic productions of all kinds have been chosen with the best taste, and admirably set off the apartments.

The Dining Room

The Dining Room is a lofty and spacious apartment, richly decorated, and adorned with choice works of art, and rich mouldings in gold and white. The ceiling particularly attracts attention, the decoration of the same having been carried out with great skill and taste by Italian workmen in 1760. The plaster figures in relief, representing Aurora in her chariot, from a very graceful design, is a work of art not frequently to be met with, the execution of the work being of a very high order. The walls are also decorated with some very fine pictures of ancient ruins by Dahl, besides family portraits and busts, the latter including a bust of Homer which is considered a particularly fine one. Altogether this apartment is justly regarded as one of the finest in the house. In the ante-room are also very fine busts of the great Admiral and his wife, by the celebrated sculptor, Roubilliac, Chinese paintings on glass in Chippendale frames decorating the walls.

The Red Drawing Room

The Red Drawing Room is another very handsome lofty apartment, 46 feet by 28 feet, richly decorated, with ornamental ceiling. Amongst the very fine pictures are three excellent portraits by Sir Joshua Reynolds, one representing Admiral Lord Anson, another the Hon. Mrs. Anson, and the third, Admiral Sir Charles Saunders, who took part in the memorable voyage round the world. A hunting scene, painted by Webb of Tamworth, in 1827, is also very fine and justly admired, the more especially as it depicts the first Lord Lichfield, Master of the Atherstone hunt, with several of the members of the same.

The Blue Drawing Room

The Blue Drawing Room is somewhat less elaborate in respect to its surroundings, but is nevertheless beautifully arranged and decorated, and bears an especially cosy aspect.

The Corridor leading to the Drawing Rooms

The corridor leading to these two rooms commands a fine view of the latter, and is enriched by cases of choice china, which formerly occupied a place in the Chinese house, but were removed to safer and more suitable quarters.

The Saloon

The Saloon is the largest room in the house, and is furnished in the highest style of art, and with exquisite taste. It is 54 feet long by 22 feet wide, being supported by twelve columns. It contains some pictures by celebrated Masters, and is altogether a princely apartment. Amongst the pictures is a large oil-painted portrait of the first Earl of Lichfield, Thomas William Anson, Ann Margaret, Countess of Roseberry, and George Anson, Major General and Commander in Chief in India. This was painted by their mother, Viscountess Anson, a pupil of Gainsborough, the great portrait painter. A shooting party at Ranton Abbey, near Eccleshall, by Sir Francis Grant, is another splendid picture, which includes portraits of the Earl of Uxbridge, Earl of Sefton, Earl of Lichfield, Viscount Melbourne (Prime Minister of that day), and Viscount Anson. A picture upon which Lord Lichfield naturally places great store, is an engraving of Her Majesty the Queen and the Duchess of Kent, which was presented to his lordship by the Queen in 1897, as a memento of her visit to Shugborough in 1832.

The Library

The Library, a long and comfortable room, is divided by an archway richly ornamented. It contains a wealth of books, and on various coigns of vantage* are busts of ancient and modern celebrities, including various Emperors of ancient Rome, and busts of Francis, Duke of Bedford, by the celebrated Nollekins, and of Thomas William Coke, Earl of Leicester.

* A coign of vantage is defined in the O.E.D. as a 'place affording a good view of something.

The Earl of Lichfield's Sitting Room

In Lord Lichfield's Sitting-room are several specimens of fine art in the way of portraits and pictures. The most interesting feature, however, is a picture which represents Admiral Lord Anson's capture of the Spanish galleon. The name of the Spanish vessel was the *Nostra Signora de Cabadonga* and it was commanded by General Don Jerouimo de Montero, a Portuguese, renowned for his skill and courage. The galleon was much larger than the *Centurion*, and contained many more men and guns. Nevertheless, in the action which ensued she had 67 men killed and 84 wounded, while the *Centurion*, commanded by Admiral Anson, had only two killed and seventeen wounded, all but one of whom recovered. The action was the more remarkable, inasmuch as the galleon had been waited for during eighteen months before *Centurion* could come up with her. The picture represents the two vessels side by side, and beneath it is the sword of the Spanish commander, which was surrendered to the Admiral.

The Countess of Lichfield's Boudoir

The Boudoir of the Countess of Lichfield which is adjoining is a cosy and comfortable room, arranged in the best taste.

# APPENDIX THREE

## An Invitation to a Society Wedding

An Invitation to a Society Wedding in 1895

The Countess Dow.ʳ of Lichfield
requests the honour of
Miss Philpott's
presence at the Marriage of
her daughter Edith,
to Captain Lionel F. King~Noel,
at St. Michael's, Chester Square,
on Monday April 29ᵗʰ,
at 2 o'clock,

And afterwards at
78, Pall Mall

An answer is requested.

# Index to People

# Index to Places